BRICKBY BRICK

BUILDING WHEN YOU'RE BROKEN

DYLAN HOUSE

Brick by Brick

Copyright © 2025 by Dylan House.

MILTON & HUGO L.L.C.
4407 Park Ave., Suite 5
Union City, NJ 07087, USA

Website: *www. miltonandhugo.com*
Hotline: *1- 888-778-0033*
Email: *info@miltonandhugo.com*

Ordering Information:
Quantity sales. Special discounts are granted to corporations, associations, and other organizations. For more information on these discounts, please reach out to the publisher using the contact information provided above.

Library of Congress Control Number:		2025902350
ISBN-13:	979-8-89285-338-5	[Paperback Edition]
	979-8-89285-467-2	[Hardback Edition]
	979-8-89285-337-8	[Digital Edition]

Rev. date: 01/16/2025

Matthew 7:12

In everything, treat others as you would want them to treat you, for this fulfills the law and the prophets.

CONTENTS

FIRST EDITON: MONTH

INTRODUCTION

LAYING A FOUNDATION

There are deep rooted questions when it comes to building something that lasts. Whether it's a home, a relationship, or maybe the foundation to a happier and more rewarding life. It is easier said than done when it comes to our future, because many of us are still fighting battles in the present, or regrets of our past. The average person might argue it is too late to start over, or that there is no way to fix the foundation you currently have.

Within the pages of this timely and inspirational book, I will be sharing blueprints that I have discovered to build a foundation that aligned me in my relationship with God and helped me to walk forward in a different fashion while holding the crumbs of an old foundation as a lesson learned. My spiritual journey has been an evolving large piece of my story that is controversial. God has made the largest impact in my life, and for those I encountered. Thousands of people argue there is no higher power, or that God is not real.

This book welcomes people of all beliefs as I stand on the basics of good values and principles I try to follow while doing it imperfectly and broken just like you.

Religion has become a hard topic that people run from. Beating you with a bible is not my purpose on this earth. A Religion vs a relationship with the creator are two separate topics completely. This book highlights the way to a better foundation built on simple moral facts that have been long forgotten.

Our country was built on the belief that God knew best. Through these pages, it is my ultimate hope to challenge the norms when it comes to creating something new in America and inspiring a change that is built on common shared values and truths.

This incredibly unique book will undoubtedly reach the deeper parts of your heart and leave you feeling inspired to build a better foundation of your own. These heartfelt written words will reveal fundamental truths you will never regret reading. My mission is to challenge all who read it, to keep an open mind and heart as I try and reach you no matter where you are on your journey.

Looking back at my own broken foundation, I realize I was a man who built my life on the sand. As a result, I have learned valuable lessons that are worth at least a glance. It is my wish for you to light a renewed passion for change in your soul and break down the walls of failure at last.

In conclusion, you will be inspired by these pages and motivated to climb that mountain looking at you in the face, or the darkest of valleys below.

Most importantly, you will finally get the chance to feel understood in a world where nobody truly takes the time to understand.

You are reading this as you try and navigate through the many twists, turns and trials of your own life. I still believe anyone can rebuild, no matter who you are or how bad it looks right now. One brick at a time, and one page at a time we will lay a new foundation together. *The heavy hitting points in this eye-opening piece are found in bold letters so you can come back to them as reminders. It is not about me as much as it is you! I believe the best is yet to come.*

THE BRICK OF BELIEF

People always say seeing is believing, but what if you are someone who stopped believing because of what you always saw? If all you ever saw was pain, I can relate because my life has been a series of painful events spread out over 26 years. Admittedly, in my own experience I kept trying to build a foundation as the storms continued hitting my life and blowing over the already broken foundation I had. What if everything we believed about success was fundamentally flawed?

Belief is like a crucial brick in the foundation of our lives, and it often cracks first under pressure.

It is the path to trusting relationships, and the road to the greatest comebacks after the worst defeats. Believing in the word believe is a task of its own. Living out the true meaning of the word is a mountain most people will not dare to climb.

There have been moments in my life where I was left wondering: where has belief got me? As a result of this mindset that I had allowed to creep in, I found myself looking over the cliff. Without much time to decide if I was going to jump off the ledge, *God spoke from the bottom of the mountain into my soul, but I still could not hear him.*

Jesus was hanging out in the valley calling me into something expansive and much deeper. Where you truly find God is at rock bottom and not pride rock. Walking through the darkest seasons of my journey, thinking the light at the end of the tunnel was near became the moment the sun went down, and the road only got darker. The common ground we all share is the simple fact that the darkness in our lives can feel never ending!

I was saved and baptized at New Spring church in Anderson, South Carolina in 2017.

With the launch of second chance church, led by a noble man himself pastor perry noble, who has taken church to the next level and won my attention when it was just a live stream.

When perry made the comeback of a lifetime in his return to do what God called him to do, I began to take a new turn in my relationship with God witnessing the boldness of preaching unfold in a movement for misfits and those who feel like they don't belong in a church building. I'm quite familiar with the feeling.

Every winding road looked straight, and it always does until it takes another sharp turn, on to catastrophe lane. I started to find out how wrong I was about this whole picture unfolding before my very eyes.

My beliefs will remain a large part of this chapter because without them, I would not be here today. God became my ultimate hope and hero in my story. *I share my faith with the world unashamed. As your friend no matter who you are, or what you believe it is my goal to show one person just how far my beliefs have brought me. Believing in a spiritual victory, which focuses on inner work and self-reflection has allowed me to achieve lasting results. I will reveal more about my relationship with God as we go! (Matt 6:33)*

There are thousands of unheard voices that feel like God is up in heaven having a laugh in the recliner chair watching the madness in their life unfold. Where is he? Believing in an invisible God has been a controversial topic and a topic of debate for centuries in the face of a cruel world where it seems the bad guys always win. As you continue reading, I will begin unraveling what I have learned about the very real and two-way relationship I have been blessed to build, with the creator. Any relationship you build involves demanding work, admitting your mistakes, dedication, and a forgiving spirit. Reflecting on my experiences has led me to believe everyone needs a hero. Especially, if the people around you called you the villain when all you were trying to do for so long was the so-called right thing. My question is, who remains the hero in your own life? Not all heroes wear capes. Psalms 16:3 states "The godly people in the land are my true heroes! I take pleasure in them!" In fact, most believers in God are viewed by the public as people who are not in touch with reality. Believing in God has become a mental illness in the eyes of people who simply cannot understand how real he is.

However, the truth is that our reality is not what it seems. Heros come in several fashions. My cat is the other hero in my life, and he is the king of his own jungle in my mom's backyard. A hero could be a significant other, or that one friend you can always call late at night when everything is turning upside down!

I sit here thinking about this quote I found; that defines the truest definition of a hero. It reads *"To be a hero is to be unafraid to stand alone for what is right." Doing what is right from my viewpoint is taking the path less traveled.*

Going back to our first discussion, *the Brick of believing finally broke when you stopped believing in yourself.* To the person that is tired of watching their dreams come crashing down as you build the dreams of others, I understand you. Likewise, I also understand if you are that person that sits there blaming yourself for certain things that other people blamed on you. It took countless hours writing this to be that friend cheering you on. I would not be here today without the belief of God being the ultimate source of my strength, which has surpassed all my expectations to say the least. *If your biggest fan and supporter was always the spirit inside of your heart that told you to keep going, that is something no dollar can buy, and I can certainly relate! The truth is, I have come back from several setbacks because of my beliefs. Also, I refuse to take the credit for all the success I've been able to build in the midst of many so-called failures and setbacks.*

To expand on the struggle of belief, it feels like we are in a constant cycle of self-doubt and fear of what others think. This is a mental rut and a trick straight from the enemy's playbook. This mindset of doubt and fear holds us back from unlocking the door that leads to freedom. We end up finding ourselves asking questions like why doesn't anyone believe in me? These questions can steer you into trying to fit into places or social groups you never belonged to or cause you to chase a crowd that you feel invisible in. It's hard to live in a world where the task of trying to fit in starts on your first day of school. To elaborate, you may find yourself turning into someone that is truly not who you are because of rejection. *Rejection and the seeds of doubt are planted when someone else tries to project their darkness and insecurities within themselves, onto you!*

When you are rejected take that as a sign you're being redirected.

Let me shoot the honest cold breeze with you for a moment since lukewarm breeze seems to be a trend.

The world will do anything to see you give up.

People would rather drag you down, instead of doing the inner work needed to heal from within. Looking inward by self-reflection and looking at our own flaws is essential to helping all of us find our very own unique talents, and gifts.

Changing what we have the power to change about ourselves. before looking at the lives of others is another way to put it. Competition with others is not on my bingo card while behind closed doors, a game of uno is going on as people try to swap the cards with me. Unfortunately, if you're reading this it is more than likely that you were squashed by the very people you wanted to support. Without a doubt, we can echo hope into all lives one person at a time and be catalysts of true change in America that flows beyond our borders, the borders we haven't had by the way. Believing in a better tomorrow is a common desire we all share. It takes all of us to achieve true change and hear each other at last.

Personally, it is my stance that believing in God is the door to endless possibilities.

By the end of this book, it will leave you in a more comfortable space to reach your own conclusion. A toe in the water was never going to teach me how to swim, and only clocking in at my job would never get the job done.

Commitment to success has been a strong motivator in my life because it gives me a sense of completion and satisfaction when I achieve my goals! Having an intense sense of commitment became a pillar for my ability to believe even when I missed the mark myself. The truth is when you are committed in your mind, it leaves no room to turn back. ("your too far to turn back now.")

Everything you are reading can feel like a lot to take in during one sitting but trust me, building Brick by Brick truly means building day by day. *Building Brick by Brick is a natural process, where falling back down constantly is proof you are quietly rising higher.*

I don't want you to feel bogged down right now, because even though I can make one point after the next, you need love more than anything else. Maybe your soul is crying for a voice that understands how you have been feeling lately. *Laying down a fresh brick of belief requires patience with yourself!* To be fair you just need someone to hear your story and listen to you for once. Yet, you are reading this because it could be that nobody will take the time to listen to your deepest cries!

I just want to be honest with the reader and reach you where you are in your journey. Honesty is hard to find but let us be honest with ourselves for just a moment. Believing to make it through one more day is hard enough when the world feels like it is on your shoulders, and when the odds are stacked against you.

Heavy weights are on the minds of many people who see the mess in the world for what it has become. The shear disbelief in what I have seen has been the engine driving me to believe in something better. In our own foundations, our belief systems tend to break along with our confidence.

Having a building mentality when it comes to building anything requires you to imagine you are already looking at the finished work.

Notably, *the power of belief is like a web that is connected to many qualities that take time and practice building. Believing creates confidence in other areas of your life that manifest physically down the road with being persistent. There is not one body builder that stays in shape by quitting his routine and habits. Likewise, Tom brady did not win seven super bowls by skipping every practice.*

During times when I stopped Believing in myself, I awakened to the fact that my self-confidence had hit the brakes too. Throughout my life, the only time I was one hundred percent confident was holding my beer on Superbowl Sunday knowing the greatest man in sports was only getting better with age. On the flipside, I am not sure if I can watch the chiefs bring home a ring every season, so something must be done about that situation. Before you shut the book because of how hypocritical it might sound, all I am saying is at least tom allowed a team or two to win one, he did not have to. I am a die-hard fan of Tom brady and the New England Patriots.

Theres nothing better than yelling at the television for 20 years. (Minus about 3 years as a steelers fan, but the steel city can win my heart too. I still love those fans to this day!)

Brady continued to dominate the league while being counted out before he could even find a pump to put air in the ball. Watching every Super Bowl became a tradition for me. I might be willing to place a bet on that perfect Sunday game if my favorite quarterback is holding the ball. If Brady is not throwing the Ball I will save my money, which also means I will never bet again!

Have you ever bet on yourself when nobody was willing to bet on you? If your name were in Vegas right now, how much money would you tell the world to bet on you?

I've bet on myself, but I didn't truly win the battle of belief until I put all my chips on king Jesus. *When God gives everyone a chance to hold the game winning ball it is too good to fumble or leave in the locker room.*

God is the reason for my victories. I have learned though; a true winning mindset starts with humility. I am humble enough to admit I am not better than anyone. I cannot count on two hands the number of mistakes I have made in my life! I want to journey back with you to the football discussion because there are perfect parallels between football and our life. I began to change my perspective when I finally figured out the ball was in my hand. The problem was I just never thew it. Instead, I became a linebacker protecting everyone and taking all the hits. Soon enough, I was fighting every battle imaginable for others that simply were not even mine to fight. To put it simply I burned out! Maybe putting the football down and picking up a glove and a baseball is the best way to learn how to throw a strike.

Burning out is a silent burn. It's the kind of burn you don't see until you're so tired you have forgotten who you are. Piles of societal stress and the American dream that has been pitched to you is the biggest curveball to ever miss the corner edge of home plate. Life has been throwing you curveballs as you have been swinging at every ball with a broomstick to finally hit one ball over the fence, in your desperation to see your dreams come true.

Suddenly you find yourself wiping your tired weary eyes.

After all the battles, all the internal war, and all the hurt, you tip your glass upside down to see it's not even half empty but completely dry. Maybe life doesn't feel like a glass, but rather a paper cup you can't even put water in anymore, because it's been crushed by the weight of the world on your back.

Nobody sees the silent nights, where silence and the fear of what tragedy will hit your life next begins to creep in. In times of burnout, we run towards rest. Resting for me at times meant putting down everything, literally! Resting is a big part of growth as individuals, communities, and nations.

Growth never stops in our lives, from an infant to the time you lay your head down for the last time changes abound. Along the straight and narrow path, we carry the heavy weights of others and become champions of our own kind in the corner of the ring standing with the gloves still on after the lights go out. The cross we carry isn't just ours, but the cross of our friends. Imperfectly, we keep pushing towards the high calling of the lord knowing the payout is a life worth living!

As I always say "Carrying the team" comes at a cost mentally, and a cost most are unwilling to pay. Furthermore, always keep this fact in mind: Your mental health is not for sale even when you feel like other people are putting it on clearance.

Sometimes we truly feel like we are always up against the wind. Seeing adversity from a clear perspective is knowing that the wind that goes against you simply means there will be more air in your lungs, and more wind in your sails.

Our flight today, departing from "trials that come out of nowhere" will be landing shortly in a place called "success that can't be stopped." Prepare for takeoff! One of the most profound henry ford quotes reads "When everything seems to be going against you, remember that the airplane takes off against the wind, not with it." You may find yourself feeling like an outcast if you are walking your own way as the world walks theirs.

Going against the wind will always land you in a place where your voice feels silenced.

It truly feels like a place where nobody will hear you out! Another fact about belief I have seen is, believing in yourself when nobody believes in you makes the task feel impossible.

Believing in anything is hard when it is what is right and not many will stand by your side when you are doing the right thing!

Painfully we cannot even believe how old we are. Seeing what is on Tell a vision is hard to believe or watch anymore.

I don't know about anyone else, but cable TV isn't worth the asking price anymore. We are in a time in the United States and the world where trust is out the window. I do not know who opened the window, but the trust is gone.

Trusting is a big part of belief that is withering away by the minute. With an elevated level of integrity, I believe dating could have a higher success rate along with marriage. Children that are given a fighting moral chance will succeed. I believe children now can be led in a direction that will lead to less crime in 10 years or even 5. If America were a nation that addressed bullying, and addressed how God is a factor in success and not just academic achievements, the world would change. *Integrity and honesty lead to trust, trust leads to belief, and belief leads you to building stronger relationships built on stable slabs.*

Right now, I am believing for a raise at Dunkin Donuts and believing for that is the closest thing to a hail Mary ball. A constant problem I have seen repeatedly throughout my journey is, *you cannot build a good foundation with paper! Increasingly, I have been observing Money being mistaken for stability. Most people believe Money is the fix to all problems. Money leads us down a path thinking that is what will save us, and it is the foundation for revenge in most cases where simply talking could fix it.* Money seems like the most stressful topic in marriages, and it is the storm many couples did not see coming, or maybe truthfully, they did.

Together we will be shifting gears and putting a strong emphasis on finances because money and belief go hand in hand during the most expensive world we have ever seen.

Finding a healthy balance when it comes to finances is a challenge when the middle class is now closer than ever to being homeless.

There are two certainties about having material things because I experienced them both! *Either you have it all and sometimes you forget to appreciate all that you have, or you lose it all and realize that all you had did not really matter in the first place. It is when you have nothing, or you are on the verge of losing it all that you value everything and start believing!*

However, it should be noted that it is not just a better financial situation that people are struggling to believe in. From A to Z, there are 23 letters in between we are still trying to figure out. Since some people claim to have it all figured out, they probably didn't make it past this point. Just know, I am not claiming to know it all either! I can only share with you what I know based on what has worked for me. My story is evidence and proof that there is success still to be found. How I managed to navigate through the impossible in real time is proof that God will use his people to do his greatest works through. {Proverbs 15:22}

The health of a nation improves when the health on an individual level is not in rapid decline. Now more than ever the struggle to speak positively has become increasingly hard when all we ever hear is sad news. *The words we speak have the power to shift our beliefs and can change the overall trajectory of the path we are on.* Being positive shifted my beliefs when I took the victim mindset I adopted and started speaking victory over my situation.

Challenges that arise day to day are an attempt to knock you back into a negative mindset, and back into a lower reality that keeps you focused on physical battles. The invisible enemy we all fight thrives best when you are feeling trapped with emotional, mental, physical, and financial chaos.

The shallow three-dimensional realm will throw a living hell at you to keep you from hitting a level up in your spiritual journey, a level up so big that it will manifest itself physically. Your ability to believe and achieve takes a level of self-belief, belief in God and eyes to see that everything you are looking for externally, you already have within you. Your talents, gifts, potential and true light is waiting to shine.

Honestly, *unlocking the truth of who you are in gods' eyes creates a threat to a shadowy world. The invisible enemy stops at nothing to keep you away from the joy that is already yours. The enemy is on a mission to steal a joy that was never his to steal and only yours to hold. The battle for the mind is where the battle starts, and where it ends. Battlefields of belief are warzones of physical challenges to stop you from unlocking the spiritual factors of yourself hidden within.*

The drop zone of spiritual warfare does not start on a flying bus with a balloon on top, but rather it starts with trying to live by the holy word of God, and in a way that honors others. Challenges that arise, that are meant to break you will be your slingshot to new heights with king Jesus. Challenging situations that I have been met with along the way. helped me recognize the power of the words I spoke to help me come into alignment with my body, mind, and spirit. Painting a constant rainbow in the sky is not realistic, I understand you! In contrast, it has been vital for me on my journey to face the darkness and negativity head on by speaking the undiluted truth. Society labels the ones who continue to fall, but it is in those defining moments and how you stand back up that tell the truth. Falling back down in this old world is proof you are moving forward.

Having harsh difficulties made me envision my life differently and wake up to a harsher reality without the smell of coffee, but the smell of some more sinister attacks coming my way.

Standing on the battlefield of belief is an everyday fight where every thought, action, and word you speak is trying to come into alignment. The man in the mirror song by Michael Jackson is worth a revisit in 2025!

Every day I do my best to take steps towards looking at the things I can change about myself. The ultimate competition starts with looking at myself. Becoming better as an individual is my goal, while others would rather talk about who I was yesterday or 5 years ago. When people only want to talk about a version of you that no longer exists is something you have faced in life. I give all glory to God above, for helping me to see the harsh truth. (Matthew 5:1-12)

My mission is to become a positive force, not only by speaking positive, but by taking more positive strides that align with my beliefs and walking through darkness with my head high.

Speaking positively helps us believe and believing helps us be positive. Interestingly they are both linked. It is always easier said than done and I can say that from experience! It truly takes practice and catching yourself when you start slipping back into a negative mindset. Believe me, I am not exempt from falling back down. When the dreams in your soul are bigger than the flames of hell you are walking through today, then your reason to keep going is bigger than the evil trying to stop you. Focusing on your dreams while being realistic and honest with yourself when you fall back down is an important part of why for me personally, I have never given up. What I want for my future is bigger than the mistakes I made today, knowing tomorrow is a chance to take another step towards the life I want. Remember, that those dreams deep within your heart, are built one day at a time and one positive word at a time.

Taking leaps of faith can sometimes feel like the only option left. Life has its own way of putting us in situations where the only logical choice is to walk the plank and jump. Whether you jump into deep uncharted waters doing a cannon ball, or a dive, there is not much time to decide if you're going to Sink or swim.

My dream was to write a book that would change the world one person at a time. I did not believe I could truly sit down and type for hours on end, while learning the formats, and putting the good in my soul down on to paper at last.

This is also not the perfect book but swinging on strike two is better than not swinging at all! (My life summed up in one sentence)

To close out this beautiful chapter, there are some particularly important things I want you to hold near to your heart. You deserve to know this about me; my life did not change until I reached the very end of myself! Of course, that is not the case for everyone.

At times, a long silent pause is key to finally seeing life from the shattered perspective of the broken. My Life changed for me when I stopped doing it my way and started trusting God to have his way in my life. Some might be asking when did this happen because the last time I saw you, you were doing this or doing that. The truth is. the messiest stories of people who we see as saints today that came straight from the bible, were people who also faced building while they were broken and royally blowing it in life. I am not writing this to make an excuse. but if you read to the end, I will be wearing my mistakes, because the blood of Jesus is enough to cover it. Putting on the judge robe is not my job but the more I look around, wooden mallets are a top ticket item because we have more judges than Jesus Christ. In my view, it is so much easier to let God do the judging, so I do not get judged by him for doing it to others. My hope is that we all put our microscopes away when it comes to looking at someone else's life and find the nearest mirror.

Humbly I admit it is never easy to be Christian. It is a constant learning experience were falling back down is a part of building in an upward direction.

Surrendering to the fact that someone much higher than me had a much better plan is what changed my life forever.

If you are in a season where the walls are caving in, that is truly the best time to believe. I am telling you from experience! I remember when I was emptying the only pack of water on the floor to be able to flush the toilet. It was at that moment I asked, why I was paying for water when it should be free? When I tell you this was the very beginning of another 4 years of disasters, I mean it! I continued to focus on building others, and not myself. Trying to build relationships and tangible, visible success while keeping God in the background, didn't pan out for me.

Thinking I was okay because I was "saved." was a path that didn't lead me to transformation. I know what lukewarm bath water feels like, because I soaked in it for seven years and got nowhere! God deserved center stage in my life but unfortunately it took 25 years to truly find him and put him back where he belongs. Chasing physical success, and love from what I could see became my downfall, while not realizing true love came from what God had already placed on the inside of me. Never go down without a solid humble fight by Fighting for what you believe in and always remember to fight for what is right. At your lowest point, when you cannot find a reason to believe any longer remember this:

Life cannot get much lower than this. I am writing this for Someone who hit rock bottom a long time ago, who built their life using the stones other People threw.

To conclude, the eye of the storm is the only place where you can see a crack of light shining through. Also, *the biggest threat to any foundation is the storms that hit us when we are doing our best!*

It's time to raise the sails, load the cannons, and prepare for the thick black clouds that loom. Theres no storm we cannot overcome together; Into the storm we go!

BUILT TO WITHSTAND THE STORM

Pirates of the Caribbean, my favorite movie ever. The thrill of ships firing back and forth, the chaos of the raging seas, and of course the way Johnny Depp stumbles throughout the whole two hours of each movie. This leads me to a question, and please do not blame the rum when I ask it. (Jack Sparrow drinking rum). Are you stumbling through this storm in life?

Take a second and think about the true answer to this question and if you are not okay, stay with me! *Some of you are in a storm with absolutely no boat. Many of you have been sinking in the waters of life and the majority feel like they have already drowned.*

Watching the hearts of people grow weary and tired has been hard for me to watch in silence. I have battled hundreds of times in my own struggles, to keep the fight alive within myself. The warmth of the sand may seem like a faraway distant land, and it can continue to develop into feelings of no hope.

During Countless seasons of my life, it felt like the direction of my quest to finally reach the shore was like watching a broken compass spin in the same circle a million times over. I have found ways to ride the waves of each passing storm in my own life. Meanwhile, scooping out Buckets of water to keep the Ship from sinking.

The truth is tides do eventually turn.

You start to realize your life is a collection of battles that were put there to make you a stronger version of yourself. You the reader, are Refined like gold that got tested with heat. *At times in my story, I have asked myself the question everyone asks: Who shuffled the cards dealt to me?* I'm here to say that those lower numbered cards you are holding were to show you that you didn't need an Ace to win. *The key to winning is playing to the end no matter what cards you are currently holding.*

Playing with a bad hand causes many people to fold too soon. A harsh wind can blow all the cards and the whole game right off the table.

In addition, *harsh experiences can give us qualities that can make us better people, but on the flipside can give us scars we end up trying to heal ourselves!*

How we respond in moments of defeat can inspire real and lasting change and lay the foundation for generations to come. *I'm talking to the individual that understands peace has no price tag. You're in a search for peace within and Peace you never found!* What does peace look like to you? Is it the stillness of the nighttime sky and watching the stars? For me, I find peace writing. *Taking the time to be alone is my healing and the ultimate source of peace.*

Often, I enjoy playing some ambient music to add the calming touch when I'm writing. Typing this book has been an incredible journey that is allowing me to dig deeper into my heart and let out what I have kept inside me for so long!

Starting a process of finding peace in your storms begins with looking within the dark corners of your heart you try ignoring to feel comfortable. I've found out the hard way, that the storm raging within us is the worst one and the most destructive. *Also, making peace with your enemies is the blueprint to your own happiness. Jesus left that blueprint in his word for all of us to learn from.*

Forgiving everyone you feel has wronged you, allows you to have unthinkable joy in the middle of your storms. Help me grab the wheel of this ship as we change directions for a moment and talk about the voice of God. Finding quiet alone time during the day or at night, is where I began to hear God speak.

Hearing god can be compared to a small whisper in our soul urging us to do something we cannot get ourselves to do. The lord was constantly tugging on me to let go of the storm within me. *Letting go of the war taking place in your mind and heart will break every chain wrapped around it. Letting go does not just free other people, but most importantly it frees you.* In the next chapter, we will be taking a closer look at this foundational brick of forgiveness. Meanwhile, I feel the need to address other important storms that people do not talk about enough!

Maybe, the milligrams are not cutting it, or the anxiety medicine did not work! Turning to the bottle is the next step towards the crisis in our minds. Maybe drinking made it worse, but drinking was the cheapest choice. I know this resonates with at least one person.

Finding a medication that works for you is a storm within itself. It is a storm where the public opinion becomes the badge you wear.

The stigmas slapped on patients is something I want to shine light on. Certain situations you have dealt with might have caused other people to call you crazy! *Honestly, I am here to tell you that you are not crazy. What you went through was enough to send anyone to the top floor.* Having hard conversations, and most importantly facing the harsh realities of our situations head on, is what helped me grow. Learning how to use the bricks on my back, to build a better foundation going forward became my mission. Figuring out how to be a better human is something that feels impossible in a world where everyone is on their own path. While you might battle feelings of being lost on your quest to find your path, it is vital to note that no two stories are the same. Finding yourself by working on who you are within, in the middle of the storm can be a light to guide you forward on the path you are meant to take.

Being human is truly the hardest task of all. People always abuse the line "you are only human," but my challenge to that statement is what if I could have been something else? From my angle, it seems less stressful to be a goldfish in a tank.

I do not know why I had to be born a human; why couldn't I have picked being a bird.? Nobody can go wrong with being high and not paying rent. No pun intended there but God made a variety of plants that I have found to help on this human journey. For example, lavender! Put that in your pipe and smoke it.

Giving grace to yourself is essential to your own peace and self-love on your journey! Also never forget, you did not choose the hard life; the hard life chose you!

I'd love to sit here and tell you a fairytale, but authenticity is the key to the heart and true happiness. *We all need love, good cheer and laughter. Smiling once a day may only last a second, but your smile speaks one thousand words to someone else!*

Make no mistake, the most profound impact you leave is decided by who you choose to be today. If you are doing everything in your power to stay afloat, the ship you are on is about to crash land right into everything you have ever dreamed of. *You are about to find the peace you have been longing for, and if you don't find it, it will most certainly find you in due time.* The destination is. going to be the happiest moment of your life, take it to the bank. You are not what people call you. Their mental image of you is not your identity. The misfortunes and depression you may be facing today, is not the end of your story!

A bad season does not define your true character. EVER! Withstanding a true storm takes the heart of a warrior and being humble enough to except help up along the way. I did not make it this far alone! Most notably, a real storm requires everyone to calm it! More times than not, if severe weather is heading your way you see it on the news and you prepare! You rush to the store and get what you know you will need for supplies and collapse the umbrellas. Porch chairs get tucked safely inside, to keep them from being blown away.

Unfortunately, that is not how every storm hits when it comes to our life! With that statement, I have a question to follow up with that I must get off my chest.

What if the storm that hit your finances, your life, your health, marriage, relationship, or career, hit with no warning? Did a storm hit your life with bright blue and sunny skies?

The storm of addiction showed up on my doorstep faster than any other storm. For individuals like me, you understand that broken hearts, stress, turmoil, and feeling like nobody understands can most definitely cause a self-destructive mindset.

In my story, I turned to alcohol without knowing a healthy balance. The slumber and mental fog I did not realize I had fallen into, became clear when I finally had a brutal awakening mentally in 2023. Trust me, awakening to harsh realities was life altering and a scary moment to say the least.

Drinking a few extra cold ones became my relief in moments of despair. There is nothing wrong with some cold beer but ***personally,*** I took drinking too far too often. It was finally time for me to finally clean it up and face the real problem: Me.

The truth about people who are addicted to anything is that it does not take away from your value as a person! (I cannot stress this enough)

God is calling me into and a deeper dive, into more uncharted waters in this chapter. If your wish is to keep swimming with me, you might need to pack lightly. From what I have seen among the religious world and as a follower of Christ, truth is something I cannot ignore! I am not the judge of how much anyone drinks, we all have our own personal limits and decide how we live.

Dylan did not call you an alcoholic because you drink!

That would be the farthest from the truth as I just spent time calling out myself for my own past issues.

Continuing further, certain individuals spend more time demonizing and labeling people that sit at the bar all night.

Truthfully, the people who are drinking their life away at 3 am in depressive mindsets more than likely have a story people are not capable of understanding and a story they would rather not burden someone in telling. I've been there! It is the people sitting at the bar feeling hopeless who God also loves, and the of group people I am desperately trying to reach in this section! Misfits are loved.

Jesus was the perfect example of someone who was hated, rejected and outcasted in his own town. He also drank wine. Grabbing yourself a glass after this chapter is encouraged as I unpack this bag of weights. Many followers of Christ are now able to relate to him more than ever because that's how Christians are starting to get treated! I firmly stand on the belief of Jesus being the only perfect judge and I believe his arms remain open to everyone in need of hope and change! Going Back to the main point of addiction, when people decide to heal themselves day to day, they turn to the cheapest remedy!

In a world where a beer at the gas station can cost less than a soda, and a cheeseburger at your favorite fast food restaurant costs less than a salad, we start to see where the problem lies. We also live in a world where affordable health care does not exist, and self-healing is the only choice. Instead of helping people in these storms, the world has a perfect recipe for making it worse, called a financial storm.

This is a more vicious storm where debts are piling up towards the roof and living the stable life you want is a far-fetched fable at this point. I have been in times of financial crisis, and the storm of no money is the biggest one.

A financial hurricane is the final blow in today's world when all you are trying to do is have the bare minimum. Written below is a perfect example of a system and society that keeps the cycles of storms going.

Let us look at the harsh truth together, unafraid.

It goes a little like this:

24

When you do not have enough money, you are told to work more. When you work more, you are told all you do is work. When all you do is work, you start to show it outwardly with frustration and you end up drinking more. When you drink more you are called an addict and are on the verge of losing the ones you love. When you finally stop the addiction, people call you a holy roller. When you are called a holy roller, you also get called a crazy conspiracy theorist because you just saw God doing a miracle. You then end up medicated for talking about what god has done in your life. As a result of being medicated you lose your job and get labeled at work. Suddenly, you made it back to square one but with even more debt and no job because you finally lost it all.

This is exactly the moment I put my party hat on. Putting the devil in check mate on a spiritual chess board. is something I never asked for but this devil that has been robbing me for far too long left me no choice, but to sit him down at last.

Having king Jesus on your side requires you to dance for quite a while with realities that are hard to swallow, and true darkness where the red exit sign seems broken. What you just read shows a clear and vivid picture of what the average person deals with when going through a real storm. Believing in God has become a mental illness in the eyes of people who don't understand how real he is. I would bet the farm more people know what this feels like than we take the time to understand.

These are the silent battles I am bringing to the light for the sake of better understanding. I am speaking out on behalf of the people who will not tell the unspoken facts.

This book will become a platform to ones with no voice and an inspiration to understand each other as we all face the storm of life! Every storm is different but the labels and demands we face daily create an even bigger one.

Theres nothing worse than getting to the end of the checkout line at a grocery store, and having your card decline after 150 dollars' worth of groceries are already in the bags. Struggling with money is a far too common storm most of us face day in and day out. It causes us to lose sleep and live in fear of Tomorrow.

Sadly, people cannot afford to take a shower. Being homeless and digging out of trash cans has become normal for people who once had it all in life.

While this is not the case for everyone, we are all seeing a growing number of more and more people who are still trying to choose between paying the light bill or eating. With greed in the back seat, and the "every man for himself" mentality in last place we can fix our land together.

Finally, it is clearer to see after reading this chapter that all storms weave together. It has been my hope to show you that all our storms financially, mentally, emotionally, and spiritually are all linked. Storms emotionally or financially can have us turning to another storm for relief without realizing it. In the end, there is hope and a way to prepare for a brighter tomorrow while enjoying the view of the sun shining in from the rearview mirror. *Building Brick by brick is a process, and one where forgiving yourself is often forgotten.*

Forgive yourself because God forgives you. What we are fighting is a giant, and the truth is powerful enough to make it fall.

THE LAYERS OF FORGIVENESS

When you look in the mirror who do you see? Is the person you see looking back at you someone you have never forgiven? **In critical moments, we often become our own worst critic.** Forgiving others can be harder, but mastering both is a crucial part of life that I am still discovering. Together, the walls of unforgiveness will come crashing down. I've learned that allowing the doors of your heart to open, when its seemingly closing shut is vital.

Keeping an open mind and heart is the first step in stopping the self-destruction and self-hatred we feel towards ourselves. The discovery of self-love and forgiving yourself can feel like a long journey that never ends. This is an important layer to our life and foundation that I will be using extreme caution in helping you fix. Self-love begins with a choice, to finally let go of everything you're holding on to that you can no longer change and only change what you can. My best advice to anyone is to let go of all the bags you're carrying. When I say drop those bags, I'm referring to bags you have been carrying that you were never meant to carry because you are not the town bag carrier. People make a living doing that at your local airport.

Forgiving yourself starts with you remembering the first fall you ever took when you were a toddler and forgiving yourself for that but it's too bad. You can't remember! Forgetting is the hardest part of forgiving because the memory of pain is a stain etched into our story and our lives. Practicing loving yourself, exercising, and being able to see yourself through a Lens that God has for you, is freedom. (Psalms 103:1)

Now I am giving you some perspective that will open the window to fresh wind, which hits you softer and allows you to get the fresh air you need. Time is a factor when it comes to forgiving yourself and others. Another big part in forgiving yourself is owning the simple fact that walking this journey as a human without making mistakes, is impossible! Though you may feel like you are not getting anywhere in life, remember you didn't make it this far by chance.

It is a known scientific fact that the chance of being born is 1 in 400,000,000,000,000. To put it simply, that number is 1 in 400 trillion! Those odds give me hope that I was put on this earth with a purpose despite my mistakes, and so were you! Another funny fact is you have a 1 in 300 million odds to hit the Powerball. Your odds are higher to win the lottery than being born.

Someone reading this may be honestly thinking to themselves what terrible luck I had! I'm here to say that your life, your love, and your voice is impacting someone whether they tell you, or not.

Hopefully by this point, I have become someone's favorite author and an inspiration. This book isn't a crowd pleaser but rather meant for the reader who feels like a small fish in a big pond, full of sharks. When the shadows of the past come lurking to keep you down, with a list of all the mistakes you ever made just remember, your dark past fears who you are becoming today.

A person who is changed and molded by yesterday is often surrounded by people who point out and highlight your mistakes before looking at their own. When people are Putting your mistakes on display, it is a way to hide theirs. Those same people would not want there's out in the open for all to see. We all have made a mess, so giving grace is the best way to bridge the gap between your own darkness and theirs.

I always hear people say do not look to the past. Personally, I have fought depression at various times, and it has not always been easy to do. It became clear as time went on that my bad habit of looking

to the past became my motivation for a better future. The past is the map to help us learn a better way forward.

Somewhere along the way, I gave the keys of my heart away too many times. I continued to put my heart into things that did not give a real return which caused me bitterness, anger, and frustration that I had not yet learned how to deal with. I am not here to lie to you, the constant feeling of coming up empty handed repeatedly can be a total letdown. *Receiving the short end of the stick truly helped me learn how to carry my cross. Not being forgiven by people taught me how to forgive others in realizing I can no longer expect me from everyone else.*

Forgiving others got easier for me when I knew I needed forgiveness too for times when I also made mistakes. Forgiving is the gift that keeps on giving. Nothing is worse for your health than Anxiety taking over without asking for permission. Especially, when the anxiety you feel comes from regrets of your past decisions or fear that you will not be forgiven! Here is my promise; **Your pain will turn into gain, your tears will flood into a stream of hope, and the vision you have for your life will one day become your reality. My hope for America is a love that will shine brighter than anything.**

Over the course of time, I have been set free from the pains of **not feeling forgiven by others, because that can also cause us to not forgive ourselves like we should.** We end up adopting the mindset of being unforgivable and that is the farthest from the truth! Sometimes value gets hidden in the baggage, which will later grow into many great lessons with wisdom you can one day share with someone else! I am living proof. We touched on rejection in the last chapter, but it is important to know that **rejection is also the gate that causes self-hate. Labels from others become the badges we wear knowingly or unknowingly because words do pack weight.** (proverbs 18:21) The truth is, you are only one step away from starting to heal and forgive yourself. It's time to wipe the board clean, and realize you were always enough. There will be Someone who comes along and forgives you and teaches you that **the most important thing in life is forgiving yourself**

and others. For me that person was Jesus Christ, and **I whole heartedly believe God has the perfect plan!**

Building your life is like a journey with no clear destination, and forgiving yourself is a necessary part of finding it because anyone that claims to have known the path all along is straight lying.

Furthermore, I have taken hundreds of turns in my own life that I felt were right at the time. It is my opinion that there are no wrong turns. **Hear me out; what if those wrong turns you thought you took, were aligning your future steps in the right direction towards the healed version of yourself? Taking the long way around is sometimes better than taking a shortcut only to cut yourself short in the end.**

Every step you take in the so-called wrong direction is not a mistake, but rather a fresh road being paved to guide you to a place within your soul called home. There is a story about myself that I feel compelled to tell you, that will paint you a clearer picture about a time more recently that taught me how to forgive. On this day, my life took a wild turn for the better in the darkest week of my life. In September of 2023, I sat in silence in the darkness of a room. Not just in any room but a room with locked windows that I could not see out of. I was at the ward!

Telling time was impossible! Having a clock in my room would have been nice, as it felt like I went back to the stone age. I honestly wanted to ask someone to grab me a candle and some warm tea. My ward trip made my old soul feel five times older. Drinking water never tasted so good for a week, and the same three-week-old Clemson Tigers newspaper became a daily read for me. It talked about how they won a game. It would be nice to see more newspapers like that one.

The icing on the Cake was that I had the best bed you could dream of. Sleeping on a high quality, blue two-inch fitness pad with one blanket made me never want to sleep in my real bed ever again! (I am the most sarcastic person at times. If you know me, you know.) Finally hitting the lowest point ever called rock bottom was the silent jackpot. I traveled far down in life to finally hit it, but the reward is a life renewed by the lessons I learned in those dark moments! **Rock bottom is the place where you begin to change your mindset and the place where you face your demons, and where you put your past and future on a balanced scale.**

Forgiving yourself for all your mistakes, is no longer running from the person staring back at you in the mirror, but understanding who you see looking back at you was made with intention and a purpose in the image of a god who loves you enough to show you, you are still alive for a reason. The very lens you see yourself through can be unclear when it feels like nobody cares to understand you in your own small world where you are trapped by questions and what ifs.

Gracefully learning the beauty of who you are was always found within and that's why you cannot see it in the mirror! In hindsight, the ward experience was not all negative, as I got to hang out with a variety of people who appeared just as broken as me that saw eye to eye with me and indeed shared their own truths that impacted me positively.

This chapter of my story began a new process of looking inwardly at myself and it helped me to look at myself more honestly. I began to see who I really was and who I wanted to be in the future. Who I would become after leaving the ward was crucial, but I didn't see the path forward at all.

During my stay at the ward, trading milk for a juice box was the highlight of this trip that made me feel like a kid all over again! Who I wanted to be in that moment was a man that traded revenge and the thought of getting even, for forgiveness in a situation I did not create! Truthfully, it took countless months of rehashing the damage and asking God for closure while working in harmony with what I wanted.

I had 5 days of peace to learn the true posture of forgiveness and strength. My story would not have been the same without going through enough pain to allow me to see forgiveness was the only way to win! Bringing glory to God and doing the right thing was my main concern.

On the sidelines of your life, people might think they could have done better when it came to your situation. Every opinion isn't fact, especially if you have been dealing with damage head on that not everyone can see.

Dealing with trauma that is Unresolved pain within is like nail polish remover that will destroy you layer by layer from the inside out. I genuinely believe God can heal the situations in our lives through our obedience to do life his way.

Forgiving yourself and others is the only way I have found that 100% releases you from every mental stronghold. Freedom will find you when you take a single step towards healing, and that is my promise!

Moreover, we are all born with chains around us that keep us tied our whole lives from experiencing freedom and seeing things for what they are. The darkness of the world keeps us blind from finding the keys to lasting change and unlocking the truth of who we really are in the eyes of the creator of the world. At this point I have already been judged for standing with God, but it is better to stand with him than trying to be loved by the growing hateful world.

Speaking of hate, admittedly there is a mistake I make almost every day. You might want to click the seatbelt. This mistake is a major problem that I feel at least one person could relate to and it will help you to find freedom from the past! I have the worst habit of Tying my shoes too tight with knots that cannot be easily untied. I find myself struggling to untie the knots I tie. *Does anyone else have this problem?*

Our lives feel like a big knot that we have tied for years upon years and cannot seem to untie.

The Knot of our life is the reason we lie to ourselves constantly, like putting bandages on broken bones or super glue on cars. South Carolina knows all about the super glue on cars remedy, just saying. Without stepping into authenticity and finding freedom from the past once and for all, we will build more knots, lay down less bricks that last, and still trip over laces that we still cannot even get untied.

The honest to God truth is we try to fix the darkness and pain we feel, by looking for healing in every place possible, only to realize it's not anywhere but within.

Along this old dirt road called life **we try to self-heal, self-medicate, and tape up the cracks within our hearts by turning to everything but the healer himself. Jesus Christ. They say hurt people hurt people, but I declare Healed people heal people at last! I'm confident that God will bless every broken road in your life and love you through every shattered piece of today!**

LOVE-THE BRICK OF GLASS

The saying goes do not play with broken glass, so we sweep it up and throw it away Without thinking twice about it. What I find even worse is we end up building our lives with the shattered pieces of love we find along the way. Love is like the brick of glass we depend on from the time we are born. My question is, what is love? It's a loaded question that every person has a different answer to.

Love for some started out in the ninth grade. The relationship clicked and that special someone may still be by your side today. That is something to be immensely proud about, and an accomplishment to be celebrated, while for me and probably thousands of you have searched your whole life for the two-way street called love. I have tried several times to build the relationship of my dreams with the shattered pieces of my broken foundational weakness called finding love.

Personally, I have always tried my best to leave an impact on people in my journey. I am going to come forward and say sorry to the people I have hurt. As a growing and maturing adult, I have a responsibility to take ownership of the hurt I have caused others.

Admitting that I have hurt people in some way is what I am being called to do. whether it was family, friends, or women I have tried to invest in. I truly did my all to be the best thing to happen in your life. All I wanted was to be the change in your story, not realizing it was me that had to change the most. Without a doubt integrity and humility is a bridge. I am not in competition with anyone but myself and Who I saw in the mirror for so long. The person I saw daily, I did not love enough. Instability and the journey of overcoming depression were key reasons for a broken relationship life. Before I continue, I want to thank anyone who has had an encounter with me. No matter what the status was, no matter what the outcome was. Thank you for being a part of my story.

In this chapter, let us oil these lamps to shine some light on the dark corners of love we never shine light on. In my life, I have not been a perfect boyfriend, brother, son, or follower of Christ. In my past, I have fumbled the ball in my 4th down attempt to do everything right. Trying to do everything right was unrealistic.

The pressure we put on ourselves in a world that already loads us with stress and pressure gives us no room to change and no room to breathe.

We rush to love others and not ourselves only to find ourselves mishandling others because we do not love ourselves. To the perfectionists reading this, you know where I am coming from! All my experiences along the way have taught me how to love differently and showed me how to be better at each attempt to do it right. *My best advice to anyone is, do not beat yourself up if you have always felt like a slow developer or a late bloomer. The key is to Remember slow development is the best kind. (Being Human is Hard)* Within the depths of self-evaluating that I explored, I realized if I wanted things to change it had to start with me and God, behind a closed door. Spending countless hours Focusing on my own flaws helped shape me into the man I am today. The hardest job is true love, and I honestly believe that. Love is more than a full-time position that always involves balance, forgiveness, hard work, and excellent communication. It can be hard to love others when behind closed doors, we do not love ourselves!

In my experience, I have ended up trying to love someone else who is broken, when I was still trying to pick up my own pieces!

My love Lens was shattered like looking through broken glass, and trying to see a clear picture of what love truly is. Instability in the category of my finances severely changed the way others viewed me in a status and career-based world.

Having your ducks in a row in today's world isn't easy when you constantly watch prices skyrocket. Saving money has become the hardest task and the American dream is looking like a long camping trip. I truly feel like Money ruins love.

The foundation I had for so long was a foundation that was falling over time, but I didn't realize it until it all came tumbling down. I'm looking to God to help me build a new foundation and I'm still building it today.

For years, I carried my past struggles with love into my adult life. As I look back at my own instability throughout my teenage years, I realize those were the most crucial years of my life.

The truth is our lives can feel like a Test Track, but for me, my life was a literal crash course! On our life path it feels like we are constantly hitting speed bumps or completely ignoring the signs to yield.

Learning the hard way has been my greatest teacher because it humbled me in the end. I am humble enough to admit my mistakes right here on this page!

I have smoked, drank, cussed, lusted, lied, I've been to the casinos, the bars, and the club. I have mistreated people, and broke promises.

I have operated out my own desires at times. I have had anger, bitterness and piss drunk moments. I have lived in immorality and got a tattoo. I don't cherry pick what's acceptable because most of us standing before God today would feel embarrassed without a grace-based faith that moves us to extend that grace to others and a grace that's so good, there's no way you can stay the same without attempting to change towards a better lifestyle. My salvation rests in the blood of Christ since there is nothing I can do to go back and change my decisions of the past. All any of us can do is move forward. Together we will read the words of Paul found in 1st timothy 1:15. Paul says something that will undoubtedly bring hope to the people who don't feel good enough for God! He says:

"This is a trustworthy saying and everyone should except it: Christ Jesus came into the world to save sinners and I am the worst of them all"

All fall short of the glory of God.

The path of change is narrower than any other which proves the words of Jesus true. People who look at me under a microscope don't realize, I already do that to myself which is why I'm here today giving my testimony of change and trying to ignite the spark of true love by finally unpacking this box of broken chocolates. Love is like a box of chocolates, and it needs to be fixed because it never belonged in a box hidden by a flashy tag and label. We end up chasing love without first understanding what true love really is. Setting the bar higher and trying to be a better person takes work. It's the work not many see and the kind of work where people want to put a mask on us when we come out of the shadows.

Love that doesn't water down the truth is a scary kind of love, but also an inspiration as we look through the house of glass, we all have. Learning better communication skills and taking the proper time to understand someone without making a quick assumption is the best approach I have found.

My sincere desire was to be the difference in the life of my friends and my enemies by being bold in my approach, but more than anything else, fair!

I tried to love the people that viewed me in the wrong light, and I often found that people who appear to have it together are the same ones that have felt just as broken as me along the way, even if it stays buried internally.

The definition of love is often defined on a Facebook post, in the comment sections, or on a coffee cup. (coffee makes us love better too!)

Love can be defined by google quotes, performance, or popularity. People are loved because of their looks, or their money. Love is a word we throw around too often and can have an impact that can change lives for the better or ruin the meaning of it completely.

What I have seen, is Love is often based on what we receive and not what we can give!

Also, I've observed that love is almost always based on outward appearances. Love is a challenge, but in this chapter, I am going to unlock the change. As I lay down the weight of this essential building block it is key to remember I wrote this because I love you. This is the most important commandment in the bible, and the most important truth. **Buckle up your heart, because in your experience of love, you never found the safety of a seatbelt around your heart!** Love is by far the most challenging word to understand because that is all we hear and not what we see anymore. Love is a verb, and an action that has not been brought to life. Looking around us, it is easy to see the path we are on as the world is turning to hate when it comes to problem solving. **War, stealing, lying, and candy coating the truth and calling it love has been a far too common solution. When I watch the world use the word love, it is like sipping on flat soda. It has the taste, but it does not have the bubbles that bring it to life. We all want to taste good soda after we leave the drive through window.**

I truly always wanted to embody a love based on action, hard work, communication, and truth. I tried to embody love by forgiveness as well. I have forgiven at times in my life so that love and peace can move forward! The harsh truth is, I did not invent the word love or its meaning.

No man loved perfectly but **Jesus Christ who died on the cross and allowed us to see that love means sacrifice and sacrificing it all. He is so much higher than me and his ways are always right.** The best book ever written is not my book, but the one under attack called The Holy Bible. First Corinthians in chapter 13 sheds light the world needs. Love is patient and kind. Love is not jealous or boastful or proud or rude. It does not demand its own way. It is not irritable, and it keeps no record of being wronged. It does not rejoice about injustice but rejoices whenever the truth wins out. Love never gives up, never loses faith, is always hopeful, and endures through every circumstance. Doing everything perfectly when it comes to love is impossible!

I have continued to try and put true authentic love into practice while completely blowing it countless times.

Moreover, it can feel like risky business and a juggling act when you are literally throwing the glass brick of love up in the air and hoping you or the person you love will catch it! Love has been my guide in the hardest of times, it is a map to a brighter future in our homes, and a brighter future in America. Alot of you have experienced the short end of the stick when it comes to love because the stick got burned over a lengthy period of time. Dealing with heartbreak or having to be the one to walk away from something that was not right for you truly hurts either way you go. I feel this wholeheartedly as I have made some tough decisions to walk away from individuals I did love very much! For millions of people abroad, love feels like a fairytale. To women who dreamed of being a princess, it all started watching Cinderella at an early age, but you soon probably realized that is not the reality of this broken culture! Loving yourself is an important part when it comes to loving others.

There is something you should never forget:

You are not unlovable just because love never worked out. Our lives are a journey where we all have a chance to impact each other. We have the chance together to fix this shattered word. At the end of this book on the very last page will be a note straight from my journal that might help you feel understood when it comes to tears. Tears have some significance because god sees them, even when you feel they are unnoticed.

To continue, this chapter is for the person who is ready to quit love completely. If your journey of finding love has been a never-ending cycle of pain, I understand you because I have experienced love that went off the track. **In my darkest seasons, I have been the definition** of a trainwreck! **To the reader right now feeling like there is no more love left to give,** I encourage you to open your heart and see that the collection of bad experiences on your path was to teach you how to forgive the past. Finally, you find yourself in the shadows untying knots, releasing the anger, resentment, and the pain you have felt for so long! Love is the brick of glass shaped by the fire, but transparent enough to see it clearer. **Feeling loved is important, but I passionately believe hearts begin to heal when you _know_ your loved by God.**

Unforgiveness can make the brick of love break! I want people to know this: **Friends, Family, enemies, strangers and to the one reading this book, I truly tried my best to be your difference.**

Someday, whether I'm here or somewhere else, I will look back and know no matter the outcome, I did what I felt was right. And stuck to my own convictions, by making a book of this magnitude.

when you are determined to prove yourself for the sake of a god who never failed by following your convictions, and doing what you know is right, you will find there is something greater that exists beyond the shadow of fear! (1ˢᵗ John 4:8)

Releasing the lie of calling ourselves a failure and knowing that everything happens for a reason is essential for our own growth and peace. **In addition, during various times in my life I called myself a failure when it came to love, because I felt like I failed people.** Hindsight told me I was trying to learn how to do something I never created! Better yet, it was never something I could find in another person, but rather in myself viewing as is a gift I was meant to share for God's glory.

The foundation of love is one we all can build together and realizing as humans were all trying to figure out what perfect love is.

Love is something that is much bigger than our human hearts can understand! **We all are trying to figure out how to do something we did not invent.**

The truth is I am writing this to someone because I love you. With tears flowing down my eyes, I close with one statement that came from the words of my best friend and savior. John 15:13 Jesus says, "No one has greater love than this: to lay down his life for his friends." When he said those words, I genuinely believe he was talking directly to you calling you, his friend.

TIME TO REST

Racing against the clock is the story of our lives. From one tick to the next we cannot catch a minute before its gone. There are days when you plan to wake up and conquer the day, only to find yourself sleeping the day away on your only day off. In my case, the no days off method never worked out in the long haul. With 24 hours in a day, it is obvious that there are only so many times you can cut the clock.

Resting in America means getting off work at twelve midnight and getting back up to do it again in five hours. Resting tends to look like working six days straight to only have one day to recover. I genuinely believe people are tired. Trying to find time with your family for some people literally requires the whole family putting in a vacation day at the same time. People tend to miss the old days, when sitting down together at the dinner table was the norm. Unfortunately, it has now become the next mission impossible. No matter what part of life you are building, *everyone at one point or another feels the need to get off the rollercoaster so to speak!*

Throughout my life, I did not take proper breaks or time out to rest when it came to building a stronger foundation. Resting for some people means getting good sleep and resting for others means not picking up one more phone call for the rest of the week. Taking time away from all the demands of life is a crucial part of inner peace, stability, self-love, and happiness. Together, let us veer off mundane road for a minute as I tell you a story. If that is okay with you.

So, the other day I woke up a few minutes later than I was supposed to. Hitting the snooze button on my iPhone is me lying to myself at six a.m. thinking ten more minutes of sleep is going to change something.

As I continued to hit snooze, suddenly forty minutes had gone by, and my eyes were still half open. At this point, I am racing around my room with my work shirt on inside out and flying down the stairs like the Flash. **On a side note, Biden is not the only one to trip on stairs. I have taken flights down staircases I wish upon nobody.**

The express lane to the bottom of a staircase is one you never forget and the journey to the bottom requires no ticket whatsoever. Honestly, my life has felt like a staircase with only one handrail to grab: GOD.

Shifting back to my chaotic morning, I quickly found another problem when I reached the car. I was greeted with an icy window! With only 15 miles left to drive in my gas tank and a tire going flat in the front because of a screw I hit, I decided to proceed to work like nothing was wrong. My problem of being tired became a "no time to think about it" solution.

Wiping the dark circles under my eyes, which looked like I just got gloved up in the ring was embarrassing. Drinking my morning can of NOS with the music blasting while being upset with myself was not the way I wanted to start the day! Often in our own stories, we find ourselves wiping our own tired eyes and driving down the road of exhaustion when everything is inside out and too icy to see the road ahead. We rush to put on our game face just so others do not see us in our worst moments.

Taking time to rest in life means not just hitting a snooze button but truly being honest with yourself when it comes to being worn out. Finding deep rooted rest that is deeper than pillow time is better than grinding off the few gears you have left. Here is what I believe; Humans were created by God with a purpose much bigger than feeling like a machine that never stops.

Based on the facts, Jesus got tired. After years of studying, I'm thinking to myself this guy Jesus was always trying to catch a break, looking for time alone, and probably trying find the time to kick off his sandals which in all honesty, probably made him more hated.

Without a doubt, if you have just enough time to kick off your shoes and that statement is ringing a bell, listening to that toasted feeling in your soul is the better road to take.

The microwave beeps for a reason, to let you know your food is done cooking! Listening to your heart while it is still beating is better than the opposite.

The marathon in your mind can feel like a daily task of its own to manage. Furthermore, a racing mind is a race we would rather lose, than win.

Various times in my own life "bedtime" was when I clocked in to anxiety mode. My next full-time job became trying to rest. It's in our time alone we find our minds in the darkest places. The mental health crisis we are seeing, I believe, stems from a world where there is no understanding.

Furthermore, missing sleep was not always due to stress when it came to me. I grew up playing video games, so late nights on the headset with the boys is not foreign territory. Playing video games saved my life many times. Video games are a much safer way to escape for adults. Being able to lock into a reality that I could restart halfway through is something we all want in real life at times. Hitting the "delete saved data" option and pressing new game sounds good to me at least.

Being able to find something you love to do helps you escape the world you want to shut out. That is why children no longer want to get off Fortnite. Sadly, they would rather be a part of a world where they shut the bedroom door and never come out rather than to go to school and face a bullying crisis. Children today face so much more than we can understand. Truly. I feel for all the children battling daily!

Speaking up and speaking out about mental health for the next generation is a topic I will never ignore as we have watched damage unfolding from bullying 20 years ago that was never addressed properly.

The future is now and resting the mind, body, and soul is a road map to a healthier tomorrow for all people. In the end, time to rest is essential in a world where time is our enemy, which leads me to ask a more important question.

Where is the happy medium when the demands of this modern world are screaming do more?

In America, working one hundred days a week is considered healthy while for others it means survival. Making time for rest is something I hope you find in your life.

There seems to be a different kind of tiredness going on in the world, and it involves our souls and it's a tired feeling that feels like there is no amount of sleep that can cure it.

My vision for the world is people not having to go to bed depressed, or worried about what tomorrow holds knowing tomorrow is already in Gods hand. Whether it's physical, emotional or mental rest you need, trust and believe it is time well spent investing in from my perspective.

My wish for the reader is to experience the stillness of inner peace! I am going to pray to the one who I know can supply rest on the inside of our hearts and minds! True rest I believe begins at a spiritual level. What we cannot see is what we are fighting. Our worst fears and deepest thoughts take us captive silently, within us. (Ephesians 6:12)

The next page of prayer does not match every person's box of beliefs but standing on my beliefs is what keeps me unshaken. Believing in a higher power is a myth to many because maybe you were never "church material" or maybe the religion didn't accept people like yourself which made you see God in a way that wasn't accurate! Humbly, I admit I agree completely with you. *There have been seasons of my own where God seemed nonexistent.*

Speaking from a balanced perspective, bible heroes we speak about on a Sunday basis, felt the same way as some of you. After 26 years, I will proudly bet it all on a man who would die for his friends (you and I). Throughout my story, I have seen God work tirelessly so I could sleep better. In seasons of pain, I have been able to rest when it did not make sense.

Sleeping when all hell is breaking loose, only makes sense to those who learned to melt in the hands of God and sometimes, with no other choice but to seek him for help. Hell for most people has been right here on earth. My Friend, you have survived too much to quit. If you are reading my book, I consider you a surfer. You do not believe me, do you?

You do not need to live on the coastline to know how to surf a massive wave of chaos.

All you need to do to know how to surf is by trying to be a good person in a cruel world, wanting what's best for someone else and putting the needs of others above your own. Worshipping the lord in spirit and in truth will also teach you how to surf. Look no further than the flames of hell you have been surfing your entire life!

The few of us that didn't even get a surfboard had to get torched our whole lives by walking through the fire. In the end we are becoming refined like gold.

Having an open mind and making this journey conversational and not confrontational to me, means approaching spirituality with a sense that we are all still learning. With no doubt in my mind, God has restored me mentally from anxiety and depression every time it hit, and that number alone is far more times than I can count. Standing with an outsider himself who overcame the struggles of the world, and standing for someone whose name has been stepped on for thousands of years has been the greatest privilege of my life but incredibly hard work. Jesus, the name above all names is worth fighting for while trying to find rest in between the hell that' has been dished out towards me.

Resting mentally and resting in your soul is hard to find. The wounds of the past or the bad memories that are stuck on replay in your mind can steal your peace and rest.

In addition, we may not see eye to eye on every topic but I'm believing love is bigger. It is my hope no matter where you stand, that you would see it was never a religion that connected us with God but a relationship. This country was founded on the belief that God was the way to a better and more prosperous land. Abraham Lincon said it best: "Sir, my concern is not whether **God** is on our side, my greatest concern is to be on **God's** side, for **God is always right.**"

PRAYING FOR YOUR REST

Father in heaven, I pray for the person reading this and I pray for peace in their minds only you can give as they read it. I ask on the readers behalf for the healing and rest they desperately need. Mental rest is what the reader needs. They're tired of going and going. They're not sure how much longer they can do it. God they are trying to make ends meet with the bills, the deadlines and the weight of the world is on them. You know their situation and you have not left the boat they are in lord. I have faith you will lighten the load they are carrying. I pray in the pages of this book for the reader to experience a pure rest from all the burnout in their lives. I love you lord, and I thank you for working behind the scenes even when we don't see you working. Thank you for giving us the strength to keep going because it is by your grace we woke up today. You see everything that we try to build in our own strength. Thank you in advance, for the inner peace and rest you will surely give to the reader after reading this prayer! If anyone knows how draining the world Is, it your son, because he got kicked down more than anyone for your name. Righteous Father, your son knew exhaustion better than anyone. It is in your name I pray to you and with confidence, Amen.

John 17:11 Jesus prays with his disciples.

"Now I am departing from the world; they are staying in this world, but I am coming to you. <u>Holy Father, you have given me your name.</u>

A CHIMNEYS ECHO

THE SOUND OF HOPE

The echo of hope is the sound of change. Building hope is not as simple as it sounds though. The echo I'm hearing in today's world is hopelessness.

Theres an overwhelming number of people that feel like if one more domino falls in their life, it's a wrap. America needs hope more than ever right now. The land we love has become a place of true despair. All of us cling to hope when it comes to the future of our families and the lives we lead. By far, the darkest feeling and the most misunderstood, is hope. Modern day "hope" is masked by smiles and the false pictures we paint about our lives to others so that nobody can see our deepest hidden feelings. Pain and the constant empty feeling of defeat will bow today in Jesus's name. Someone right now reading this is getting ready to demolish their entire foundation and turn down a darker path. To be fair, countless people are still hoping for a cure for an illness after years of suffering, but hoping simply has not cut it. On various occasions, I have felt like it was easier to leave my hopes and dreams behind.

Feeling let down in a world that keeps holding you down is something people do not see or understand.

Breaking through harmful toxic cycles while slashing through invisible barriers, takes forgiving yourself, hoping, believing and self-love It takes everything in you to reach the next level, going from hoping to achieving. Hope has become the hardest subject to discuss and I will explain why. *Tackling this topic for me personally involves being raw and unfiltered while still sharing words of encouragement without sacrificing the truth. Hope is more complex than what it chalked up to be from my perspective.*

Additionally, having hope is a driving force that gets me out of bed in the morning. Truthfully from the other side of the coin that is not always the case, because at times the feelings of no hope kept me in bed. Hope can be as simple as hoping to make it to the safety of your bed at night.

Writing on Hope from a long-range perspective is what I feel is the best way to paint a clearer picture and actually hit the target. In my own life at various points hope has been shattered enough, to where I can honestly say I was able to see it clearer.

Feelings of hopelessness on my journey forced me to dig deeper, by believing in what wasn't even there. Believing is the action that brings hope to life while hoping, is the spark that leads us to belief by seeing the unseen.

For example:

Hoping I could draft a book became a reality for me when I believed I was already an author in my mind. I saw the cover of my book in my mind and what I wanted it to look like before I got the design. Not kidding. Believing you already have what you are hoping for is the centerpiece to the whole puzzle that Jesus spoke of in scripture.

When you buy a puzzle at the store, it shows the picture on the front of the box of what it will look like when it's all pieced together. Now, imagine for a moment you buy a puzzle at the store with a blank box and no picture of what it's supposed to look like. These thought-provoking questions may help you envision a better life for yourself. Blind and deep-rooted faith will get you to the destination when God is in first place. The puzzle you are trying to put together requires a god that already sees how the picture looks when it's finished, while trusting him to lead you in your next step towards it.

You will start to walk into alignment the moment you trust there is a better future for you made by a god with better plans than your own. Sincere hope is looking at your husband or your wife and saying we can fix this marriage because with God all things are possible. Hope is looking at your broken situation and believing in the healed future you can't yet see. Hope means even when there is no light visible at the end of the tunnel, you power up the flashlight and keep walking forward. *Hope is not being able to see the picture, but believing and knowing the pieces will fit together.*

Medical experts cannot understand the spiritual elements to a healed mind, body, and soul because for many of them, giving refills is their job. It's not just a pill that cures people, but a god who is alive that also lives in us. Please know, I'm not claiming to be a medical expert.

There is nothing wrong with modern day medicine. In fact, from a case-to-case basis success stories exist for so many people. My luck hasn't panned out in that department! It is my opinion that a designer much higher than me knows how to bring hope better than anyone.

God knows humans better than we think we do and his plans for our life will far exceed our own! God works in the kingdom department and that kingdom is within you.

We are talking about a god in heaven, ready to bring heaven down. God is in all things, which means you and I are a part of him. The kingdom being built is already within his people.

Jesus never gave me what the world had, but he generously gave me what the world didn't by allowing me to do it the world's way and finding no success. **If God can do the impossible for me, I have no doubt he will do it for you! (Matthew 21:21)**

Gods promise is to bring you to the promised land where your hopes are reality. Most importantly, the echo of this chimney we are building together will be heard and echoed for years to come. God is spirit and no one has ever seen him. The spirit of God will be your compass and the echo within your soul!

From the beginning of this book to now, all the pieces of the foundation are coming together. The view from the chimney top after a long climb is worth it. Our lives can be likened to a chimney built with no way for the smoke to escape. The stress fires that happen in our journeys create the stifling smoke that blocks our ability to see clearly and breathe the clean air we are needing. As you cut through toxicity, the sound of hope starts as an echo likened to a soft whisper.

Hope doesn't shout, it echoes a sound that carries weight, sometimes in pure silence. Avoiding the topic of hope in this book was something I pondered. Talking about hope can feel like I am pitching you a fairytale from the middle of the diamond standing on the mound. Writing about hope authentically without painting a rainbow is a task within itself. After consideration, I have realized that taking the dive into bigger issues that many are facing is my calling. Most importantly, I hope that you never give up on your dreams. My hope for you is that no matter what you woke up to this morning or what you can't get out of your mind at night, that peace will find you where you are. Excepting the things you can't change, but changing what you can is a step in building a sound of hope and an echo that will be heard years from now.

Whether you're building your life from the top down or the bottom up, nothing can stop the great plans of the lord for your life. In my closing opinion, there's no season too low for hope, and there's no height too high for shouting it out.

The echo of hope will touch many lives to come, and it starts with me. From me to you

NO PLACE LIKE HOME

What is home? Is it the place you work? some of you feel like it's about to be your car because of a crisis you're more than likely facing. Everyone has a different idea of what home is. If you find yourself building a home, it starts with a blueprint. with precise measurements, waiting to be brought to life. No matter who you are, home is a place we all want to know more about. The search for true and lasting love means home to many.

My personal idea of a home is one I build every day, that I take with me and share everywhere I go. When I imagine home, it is a place where truth, love, and forgiveness is taken off the back burner. Beyond the shadow of a doubt there is a person out there who has been in search of the true meaning of peace and comfort in their lives. Precision building when it comes to our lives is the hardest task because all of us were handed a blank blueprint to build with. We all grew up artists of our own kind from birth. Drawing up the designs for ourselves of what we wanted our life to look like! We are all building something daily and no matter what, you are holding the pen to write the better pages of tomorrow. Surviving the world and systems, we didn't create became the norm to follow. People like me understand learning the hard way. Life is the hardest journey and sometimes making sense of the bigger picture is the blur between the lines. We hit moments in our story where the measurements do not line up, and the math is not mathing. Truly, building something that lasts in life means tearing down old ideas and creating something built on the mistakes of the past. In the closing chapter of this book, it is not about how we start but how we finish. I believe in finishing strong no matter how bad it looked for you up until this point. **The biggest battle of your life is the one you told nobody about. The worst nightmare you ever had is the one you experienced**

while your eyes were open. My worst dream was watching the country I love in real time go backwards.

Mysteries, truths, and revelations about the journey we are on as humans is an evolving story that we can all impact by the decisions we make today. With my belief in God, here is what I have to say; *If I get to the end of my life and I was wrong about my beliefs, I still lived my life following the example of the greatest man to ever live named Jesus.*

He remains the MVP and Hero of every class, race, gender, community, country but most importantly the best friend in my life.

I did not write this book for me; I wrote it for you. This book is not for fame because all the fame belongs to king Jesus in heaven. I wrote this authentic and unique piece of writing I call a book to make a lasting impact on one person.

This book really took some work, some tears, some guts and some experiences in my life to be able to write about what I have seen to be true with my own two eyes.

Profits from this will be donated towards investing in something even bigger from here on home field that will help the next generation. The world is starving for change. To the ones that say do not worry about the world, are the same people hoping for something while panicking and upset when things finally hit the fan, and everyone is affected. Our world feels like it is on thin ice as we are more concerned about arguing and pointing the finger than realizing our shared human equality. On a side note, a reminder for me daily is remembering that Noah's ark did not build itself, rather it had to be built. Noah and his faith caused him to move and build something that people laughed at, until the rain of the flood finally came.

We are all born in the image of God, and we are all equally broken in a world that could not see a better way forward. Shooting Donald trump is not the answer to an already broken system. I'm sure he would like to get home safe too after a relaxing game of golf on the green. I voted for God long before a president and I do not find my answers in politics but with a God first mindset.

The closing chapter of this book may feel like a full clip, but our home is under attack from spiritual and mental unrest.

We need love more than hate, understanding more than judgement, unity over division, and a Sunday Football game having a barbecue once again with the family despite trying to always be right religiously or politically. I grew up in a world where at one point the bible got in the way of relationships and friendships I loved. It was used as a weapon to divide when God wants to multiply in our lives.

Love is the greatest commandment, and I truly have a vision for a better tomorrow. Ignoring the facts about our shared home and the things going on in our homeland is something as a follower of Christ I will never shy away from when it has affected me my entire life. Love must be bigger than hate.

Impacts we make on each other daily can chip away at hate, misunderstandings, and division.

It takes one person at a time holding the ice pick to chip away at the block of ice-cold rejection we have created. Recognizing the power of the impact and imprint we leave on each other is vital to our future. With mental health labels being printed on good hearted people faster than the item you ordered last week online, it is crucial we build this future as one nation under God. The invisible god that no man has ever seen (john 1:18)

I dream of a future where understanding is the new normal. I'm willing to lose it all writing this, and I'm willing to send it to the next level, for the person that doesn't believe anymore.

A five-star review is not needed, or a red carpet. I just hope you felt understood for the first time in your life. Missing meals and eating raw noodles in the cabinet is something I understand. My desire has been to embrace true Christianity for what it is and help someone who has been kicked out of a church chair for not fitting in the box of religion.

The next book is the one you write, and nothing can ever stop you from fulfilling your dreams. We all are authors, only some have the courage to put it down on paper at last. In conclusion, this is a book written from my heart to yours.

2 Chronicles 7:14 "If my people who are called by my name humble themselves and pray and seek my face and turn from their wicked ways, then I will hear from heaven and will forgive their sin and heal their land".

A THANK YOU MESSAGE

To all the people I've crossed paths in my life, thank you. To all the job opportunities, and the work relationships I have been blessed to form throughout my career, thank you. Thank you for truly building me into who I am today. Thank you to my family for standing in faith that I could keep pushing forward. Thank you to Oconee County for being outstanding. Thank you to Itron, Greenfield industries, and the doctors in practice who did their best to serve me.

Thank you to the whole state of South Carolina for trying your absolute best when it came to me. From every small encounter I've had in my life, to every long relationship, you made a difference. From every sour ending to every bittersweet moment of joy, thank you wholeheartedly.

The impact of one person can change a life. Thank you to my mother who has given me an example to follow as a child. My mother went out of her way to be the best mom out of the gate. She took on the biggest job of juggling life. Working 2 jobs was her reality for years, all while being unfairly judged, which doesn't help anyone grow. She has been stepped on for many years and is the overcomer herself that taught me to never quit. She raised me on moral values and principles that have shaped me into who I am today. As a woman who loves the children she teaches, she also has a profound ability to care for the sick and the poor, which is what Christ taught. she embodies love that frankly she has not always received. Thank you for being strong and never giving up as a mother. You never failed, but rather exceeded expectations while facing the constant uphill battle of life. Thank you for running the extra mile. Thank you for pouring your heart into our lives and taking on the world you were handed with passion and grace. You are the reason I'm still here and I love you forever. Nothing can outweigh the heart you have within. Nothing can separate love between a mother and son. Not the past. not the future. No external forces, mistakes, can take away the spiritual bond shared so long ago.

Finally, thank you to Milton and Hugo for not just being an outstanding publishing company,

but a friend to someone who had a vision to write a masterpiece of its own kind based on the story of my own struggles and how I managed to rebuild. Thank you for supporting my endeavors and dreams to do what I'm most passionate about in life. You have all helped me to become the man I've always desired to be. I love and appreciate you all and just know that Anything is possible with God in our corner!

Matt 19:25,26

When the disciples heard this, they were greatly astonished, saying, "Who then can be saved?" But Jesus looked at them and said, "With man this is impossible, but with God all things are possible."

A PAGE FROM MY JOURNAL

In the quiet night sky, whether the moon is hidden or it shines is proof there are stars to still see. In our Journey, we miss the details of the miracles happening before our eyes. Seasons change like a whisper, and the orange leaves that cover the hilltops make the darkest of valleys shine. Humanity as a whole has shed enough tears to fill the ocean and it is proof that water doesnt just come from the earth, but our eyes. In my imperfection i see mind, body, and spirit trying to align.

Every moment of joy makes me ask myself if the eternity god placed in our heart, is the very thing we are trying to find.

Ecclesiastes 3 : 11